Baby animals in desert habitats

Bobbie Kalman

Crabtree Publishing Company

www.crabtreebooks.com

The Habitats of Baby Animals

Created by Bobbie Kalman

For Sean, Liam, Charlie, Dexter, and Bonnie
Grandpa and Grandma love you.

**Author and
Editor-in-Chief**
Bobbie Kalman

Editors
Kathy Middleton
Crystal Sikkens

Design
Bobbie Kalman
Katherine Berti
Samantha Crabtree
(front cover)

Photo research
Bobbie Kalman

Print and production coordinator
Katherine Berti

Prepress technician
Katherine Berti

Illustrations
Barbara Bedell: pages 16, 22

Photographs
Corel: pages 1 (bobcats), 7 (top), 11 (bottom),
   19 (bottom right), 23 (bottom right)
Digital Vision: page 19 (bottom left)
U.S. Fish and Wildlife Service/Wikipedia:
   page 21
Other photographs by Shutterstock

Library and Archives Canada Cataloguing in Publication

Kalman, Bobbie, 1947-
    Baby animals in desert habitats / Bobbie Kalman.

(The habitats of baby animals)
Includes index.
Issued also in electronic format.
ISBN 978-0-7787-7725-0 (bound).--ISBN 978-0-7787-7738-0 (pbk.)

    1. Desert animals--Infancy--Juvenile literature. 2. Desert
ecology--Juvenile literature. I. Title. II. Series: Kalman, Bobbie,
1947- . Habitats of baby animals.

QL116.K34 2011   j591.3'909154   C2010-907480-7

Library of Congress Cataloging-in-Publication Data

Kalman, Bobbie.
  Baby animals in desert habitats / Bobbie Kalman.
      p. cm. -- (The habitats of baby animals)
  Includes index.
  ISBN 978-0-7787-7738-0 (pbk. : alk. paper) -- ISBN 978-0-7787-7725-0
(reinforced library binding : alk. paper) -- ISBN 978-1-4271-9600-2
(electronic (pdf))
  1. Desert animals--Infancy--Juvenile literature. 2. Desert animals--Ecology--
Juvenile literature. I. Title.
  QL116.K35 2011
  591.754--dc22

                                                    2010047669

Crabtree Publishing Company

www.crabtreebooks.com   1-800-387-7650

Printed in China/022011/RG20101116

Published in Canada
Crabtree Publishing
616 Welland Ave.
St. Catharines, Ontario
L2M 5V6

Published in the United States
Crabtree Publishing
PMB 59051
350 Fifth Avenue, 59th Floor
New York, New York 10118

Published in the United Kingdom
Crabtree Publishing
Maritime House
Basin Road North, Hove
BN41 1WR

Published in Australia
Crabtree Publishing
386 Mt. Alexander Rd.
Ascot Vale (Melbourne)
VIC 3032

What is in this book?

What is a habitat?

A **habitat** is a place in nature. Plants and animals live in habitats. They are **living things**. Living things grow, change, and make new living things, such as new plants or baby animals. These camel mothers have given birth to **calves**, or baby camels.

Living in a desert

These camels live in a **desert** habitat. Deserts are dry places that do not get a lot of rain. Desert plants and animals are suited to their habitat. They do not need as much water as animals that do not live in deserts.

What do they need?

Habitats are made up of living and **non-living things**. Air, sunshine, water, rocks, and soil or sand are non-living things. Living things need non-living things. They also need other living things, such as plants and animals. Living things find the things they need in their habitats.

Living things need water. These hyena puppies have found a puddle of rainwater to drink. Finding water in deserts is hard because it does not rain very often.

Living things find homes in their habitats. This coyote pup's home is a hole in the ground. The pup can stay cool and safe in its underground home.

Living things need food. This young roadrunner caught a mouse to eat. Roadrunners eat insects, birds, snakes, lizards, and other small animals.

Continents and deserts

Deserts are areas that get less than ten inches (25 cm) of rain or snow a year. They cover about one-fifth of Earth.

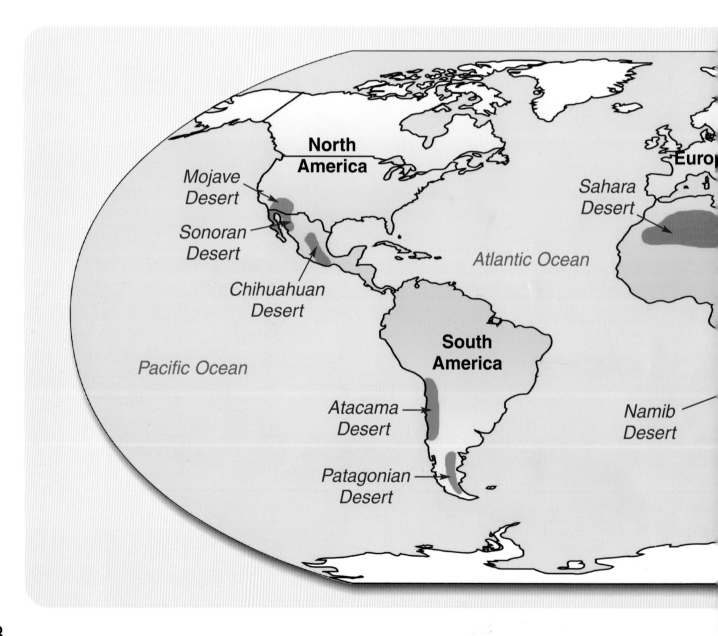

Deserts can be found on every **continent**. A continent is a huge area of land. This map shows Earth's seven continents and some of the deserts on them. Most of the continent of Antarctica is a desert. It gets less than eight inches (20 cm) of snow in a year.

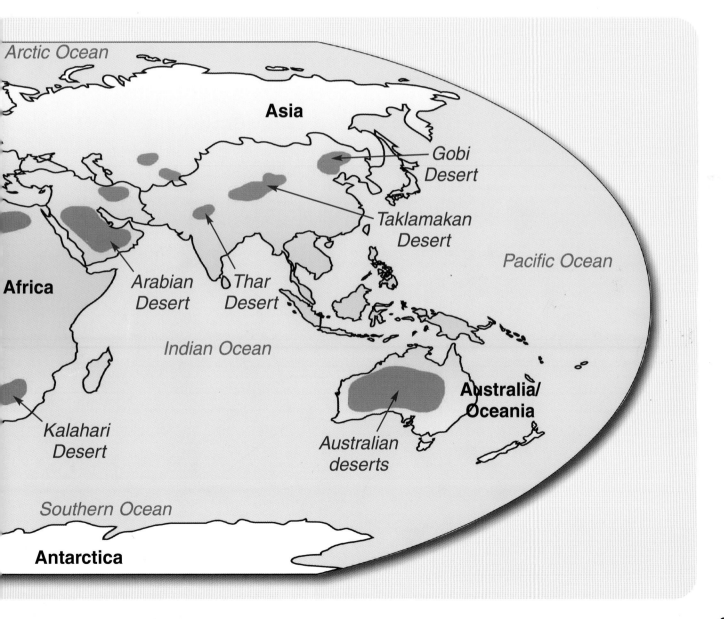

Arctic Ocean

Asia

Gobi Desert

Taklamakan Desert

Pacific Ocean

Africa

Arabian Desert

Thar Desert

Indian Ocean

Australia/ Oceania

Kalahari Desert

Australian deserts

Southern Ocean

Antarctica

Kinds of deserts

The pictures on these pages show some different kinds of deserts. Some deserts are hot, and some are freezing cold. The Sahara Desert in Africa is the biggest hot desert. The coldest, driest, and windiest desert covers most of the continent of Antarctica. Some deserts are hot during the day and cold at night. Some deserts get rain for parts of the year. The Sonoran Desert in North America has two rainy seasons.

*Some deserts have huge **dunes**, or sand hills. Dunes form when piles of sand are pushed around by strong winds. This desert is part of the Sahara Desert in Africa.*

Most of the continent of Antarctica is a cold desert. Very few plants grow there, and only a few kinds of animals live in this freezing habitat. These penguin parents and their chicks live on Antarctica.

These baby kit foxes live in the Sonoran Desert in North America. The Sonoran Desert has the most kinds of plants and animals (see pages 20–21).

Baby desert animals

These are just a few of the baby animals that live in deserts around the world. Under each animal is the name of the desert where it lives. Find the deserts on the map on pages 8–9.

collared peccary piglet
(Sonoran Desert)

hyena pup
(African
deserts)

jackrabbit leveret
(North American
deserts)

baby kit fox
(North American
deserts)

great horned owlet
(North American
deserts)

suricate pup
(Kalahari Desert)

ostrich chick
(Sahara
Desert)

fennec fox kit
(Sahara Desert)

camel
calf
(Sahara
Desert)

penguin
chick
(Antarctica)

kangaroo joey
(Australian
deserts)

A desert community

Meerkats, or suricates, live in the Kalahari Desert in Africa. They live together in **clans**, or family groups, of 20 to 30 members. Suricates look for food during the day. They eat mainly insects, but they also eat lizards, snakes, scorpions, spiders, eggs, plants, millipedes, mice, and small birds.

Suricates act like members of a community. They help one another find food, keep safe, take care of their babies, and guard their homes from danger.

Suricates live in large underground homes with many openings.

*Suricates take turns as guards. They watch for **predators**, or animals that eat other animals. If a guard sees a predator, it barks loudly or whistles.*

*Suricates are **mammals**. Mammal mothers feed their babies milk. This pup is drinking its mother's milk.*

Suricate pups come above ground when they are three weeks old.

15

Caring for the babies

Some animal mothers do not take care of their babies after they are born or hatch, but mammal and bird mothers do. Penguin and ostrich fathers also help look after their young. Suricates even have babysitters to help take care of the pups!

penguin parents and chick

ostrich mother and chicks

Ostrich mothers take care of the eggs during the day. The fathers sit on them at night.

16

Mammal mothers **nurse** their babies, or feed them milk from their bodies. This hyena mother is feeding her pups.

Kangaroo mothers carry their joeys in pouches. A joey nurses inside the pouch and lives there for about seven months.

pouch

Desert bodies

The bodies of many desert animals are suited to desert life. There is not much water in deserts. Camels can live without water for about two weeks. They can then drink huge amounts of water. Some desert animals get their water from the foods they eat. Many sleep during the day and look for food at night, so they will not lose the water from their bodies by sweating.

This camel calf gets the water it needs by drinking its mother's milk.

baby jackrabbit

What big ears you have!

Animals lose heat through their ears, which helps their bodies keep cool. Big ears lose the most heat. Foxes and rabbits in hot deserts have bigger ears than foxes and rabbits in cooler habitats.

Fennec foxes and kit foxes both live in hot deserts and have big ears to keep them cool.

fennec fox

The huge ears of bat-eared foxes keep these animals cool. Big ears also help the foxes hear insects under the ground. These foxes eat insects.

kit foxes

19

The Sonoran Desert

There are more kinds of plants and animals in the Sonoran Desert than in any other desert. **Cacti** and **shrubs** are the most common plants. Cacti are plants with leaves that look and feel like sharp needles. Shrubs are short woody plants. Some of the baby animals that live in the Sonoran Desert are shown on the next page. You can see other Sonoran Desert animals, including a coyote, jackrabbit, roadrunner, and some kit foxes, on pages 7, 11, 12, 19, and 23.

This collared peccary piglet is sleeping on its mother's fur. Peccaries eat mainly plants.

down

These baby great horned owls are covered in soft fuzzy down. Their feathers will grow in later.

This young iguana has climbed up on a cactus plant. Cactus plants are sharp, but iguanas can eat them. Ouch!

21

A desert food chain

Animals need **energy**, or power, to breathe, move, grow, and find food. All animals eat other living things to get energy. Some animals eat plants. Animals that eat plants are called **herbivores**. **Carnivores** are animals that eat other animals. A **food chain** is the pattern of eating and being eaten.

All energy comes from the sun. Green plants use the energy in sunlight to make food from air and water. They use some of the energy and store the rest.

Sonoran Desert food chain

sunlight

Plants use the sun's energy to make their own food.

A jackrabbit eats plants and gets some of the sun's energy.

When a kit fox eats a jackrabbit, the energy of the sun passes from the plants to the jackrabbit and then to the fox.

Words to know and Index

ears

food chain

Other index words